TALKING TO HAWKS

AND OTHER POEMS

HOWARD WINN

Cyberwit.net
HIG 45 Kaushambi Kunj, Kalindipuram
Allahabad - 211011 (U.P.) India
http://www.cyberwit.net
Tel: +(91) 9415091004
E-mail: info@cyberwit.net

Printed at Repro India Limited.

Many of these poems have appeared in such literary journals as *Galway Review (Ireland),Dalhousie Review, Descant (Canada), Break The Spine, New York Quarterly, Southern Humanities Review, Borderlands, Beloit Poetry Review, Xavier Review* and *Toyon.* His novel, "Acropolis," has recently been published.

Contents

TALKING TO HAWKS

I also listen and wonder
whom you talk to in that
lonely tree or in the blue sky
cloudless today and tomorrow?
does it have something
to do with the crows
circling under your tree
or following your flight
these questions might intrude
or are you embarrassed
to be asked to reveal or
are you commenting upon
the season, or the length
of the day or the chipmunk's
think they hear a god of wrath
proclaiming from above,
in tree or sky or universe,
that they are the sacrifice
to feed hatchling hawks,
and they scuttle for cover
or are you just crying
over and over that this country
is yours to lord over
and others must bend
to your will or do you
speak for someone else?
and what language is this
that you utter and can I hear it
and would I comprehend it?

A BIRTHDAY PARTY

for some one
very old
can seem
to be just
a dress rehearsal
for a funeral

IT IS HER BIRTHDAY

and the celebration focuses
on her white hair as she
has tossed her dye into
the waste basket below the
bathroom's sink and swore
to be natural henceforth
as she applied the eyebrow
pencil and the expensive
Chanel Number Five
to her shaved armpits
to provide the world with
unnatural odors of the
cosmetics stench of society

SO WHAT IS THE POINT

as old friends age and die
and the young view the world
where the ancient survivors
stand in the way of satisfaction
and the desire to acquire the
experience of thought will
action be enough to
substitute time that pretends
to be the validity of
life's messages or is it
all just an illusion of
knowing as time wins
the battle of knowing.

ACONITE

Masquerading as innocent butter cup,
yellow blossoms peer through the snow
as the first flower in my yard,
closed at first as a small yellow fist,
opening when the sun warms.
The leaves surround the failing flower
at last as Spring welcomes other buds.
Attacker of the nerves and heart,
killer in sufficient quantity,
this wolf bane slows the human heart
until all action ceases
and the lovely little harbinger of Spring
leaves the body inert,
withering as the season flourishes.
Prettiness obscures the deadly quality
of the untamable physical world.
Learn that beauty and innocence
can be fatal.
Nature does not show mercy.

THE OTHR BIRDS ARE SILENT

as the winged appetite swoops in
great circles overhead even
squirrels duck to cover or
freeze against tree trunks to
appear as part of the bark while
only the crows sail above while the
blue jays tempt destruction at
the bird feeder were appetite
overwhelms caution as if these
was a life not worth living with-
out sunflower seeds in abundance
and the jays are almost human in daring

CATFISH

lurk below the rowboats
tied to shore in the
shadows of the fun craft
revealed when those on
vacation set forth for pleasure
the innocent fish lurk in
shadows that give them
safety from frying pans waiting in the holiday breakfast
where nature and civilization
collide in the hot olive oil

THERE IS NO POEM

without a poet
even if he or she hides the work
in the language used or
not used the creator
and his life is the work
of belief or conviction
 the work is all
for there is nothing else
beyond consciousness

THE MAN FROM AMOCO

I need a drink, he said.
I really need a drink,
while eyeing the wine
glasses on our table.
No hope, I told him,
this is a wine night.
Banqueting at the 50th
College Reunion left
him very very thirsty
and very very pissed.
British Petroleum
bought up his Amoco,
headquarters moved
to London and he was
a Forrest Hills kind of fellow,
so into retirement.
Only a V. P. in chemicals,
after all, not London stuff,
and now this!
No hard liquor, either,
only red wine in plenty
to complement rare beef.
On the other hand,
he had made it in time
for this reunion.
Not everyone was a V. P.
for anything like Amoco.
Life has some satisfactions,
but he really needed

that Scotch and water.
He might have gotten it
if we had been in London.

SINGULAR PERFORMANCE

I have always preferred being a soloist
to playing in the ensemble,
the sonata instead of the symphony,
leopard or butterfly rather
than hyena or ant.
In track, I ran the 100 yard dash,
alone with my breathing and cinder crunch
under my shoes, aware of arms and legs,
or rising up over sand pit in the broad jump,
still kicking the solid ether as though
walking apart through air.
Even the quarter mile relay,
taking the baton from the second runner
and running third to keep the lead,
was a singular performance
to final transfer of baton,
leaving me gasping while anchor
struggled alone to maintain our gift
of distance.
This art is solitary sequence,
order of one mind and one fancy
while word suggests word
as steps on cinders or in air,
until we break the tape in private,
despite any crowd who watches.

THE KID ACROSS THE STREET

must be eleven or twelve.
is shooting baskets by himself.
lofting the ball toward the portable
hoop high above his head on the
edge of the driveway with no
friends to play one on one and
not even his father who sometimes
fills in at the game to encourage
his desperate son but now
there is just the incessant pop
pop pop of the ball bouncing
on the black top surface
as the kid imagines he is evading
some not nearly adept invisible
opponent and then trying a lay-up
or a long shot most of which
bounce off the rim in failure
though no one is there to observe
or judge except this young boy
and we do not know what he
thinks of himself or his dream
of that unlikely future
when the scene is a gym
the floor is polished wood
and classmates to come
applaud his dexterity and aplomb
the assurance heis trying to create
 onhis father's black driveway

A HARVEST OF ACORNS

drives the chipmunks into a
state of apparent ecstasy or
so it would seem if chipmunks
were human beings but for me
a walk is rather like a expedition
on ball bearings from great oaks
that shed leaves and these tree seeds
as summer slides into a New England
autumn that excites the squirrels
as well but the prudent rodent
buries the excess supply for
latter consumption while the
human observer wonders if
a rodent memory is a duplicate
of that of the human hoarder
will those buried nuts just germinate
and produce a grove of small trees
to be eaten by the hungry deer
who consume the resultant greenery

A SILLY WOMAN

has died or "flown away"
reincarnated as a blue-
footed booby perhaps
as her grieving daughter
puts it in announcing a
wake as she calls it at
a local pub for a party
and her friends are stuck
trying to say something
in the sympathy notes
to this daughter making
these final arrangements
without lying since the
members of this small
group are individually
ethical so even condolences
must be truthful which
makes it difficult to
write the conventional
card or note since one
cannot quite turn a daft
woman into a wise one
in the post mortem that
this celebration of life
after death partied
from three to when it
is over at the bar and grill

A VIEW FROM THE IVORY TOWER

There is no Rapunzel here but there are many others
who will gladly let down their hair
if there is a joke behind the act,
or a promotion or tenure or all three.
Clearly there are many jokes lurking
in the abstruse air of the academic
where genius is a term tossed about
as easily as juggling ten pins,
and prizes or publication can be found
it one is willing to turn over the rocks
and not mind the salamander or night-crawler
that might be revealed instead.
All in a day's work,
filling the heads of students,
like pouring milk into a glass
until it rises to the level of their eyes.

AN OCCASIONAL DEER

comes out of the woods
edging our mowed lawn
but never when it is being
noisily trimmed by the tractor
mower expensively purchased
from the local Home Depot
but usually when one of the
family is soaking in the sun
and we wonder what this nearly
a fawn seeks that drives
him from the sanctity of our
Maine woods for we have
nothing to feed it but the wild
flowers in season and if we
call out it pauses to look
briefly at the caller and then
ducks its head and retreats
into the welcoming woods
where it is the ruler and
not a temporary resident who
owns the land for the moment

WALKING IN THE WOODS

the view is bucolic as the dog-tooth
violets in bud seem to wait for
the spattered sun light to sift
down through the trees
and lure them to opening
blossoms which are really tiny
lilies between those mottled
leaves that spread under the
pines and oaks just beginning
to bud as we walk the brown
leaves disintegrating on the path
while we cannot look up at
forest primeval but must watch
our feet as we hike over half-
buried roots that seem stationary
snakes plunging in holes or
careful emerging under our feet
for such a journey into the
natural requires we watch
each step for fear of stumbling
into a fall amongst the dead
decaying leaves or the living
lilies of the tangled fallen
trees heaped at random in
this park-like wood where
dogs off leash romp and splash
in the cascading brook we hear

FORMER FRIENDS

We stopped answering Christmas cards from Mexico,
although that was the dwindled down
remnant of communication at the end of our friendship.
I went to high school with her younger sister,
even though she always claimed
to be the baby of the family.
She needed to remain that nursling all her life.
She married a charming hustler,
a photographer with genuine talent
and an eye for the scene
and the female model.
They boozed and smoked
and wrote and painted
and photographed simple
Mexican fishermen drying their nets.
While creating whimsical artwork for children's books,
they killed a bottle of vodka or red wine in one night,
insulted one another and their friends
although they did not seem to
remember the next day or
the next week or the next month.
They threw parties for the Sun
and celebrated the solstice as if for a friend or relative,
but lost friends and relatives one by one,
through death, disappointment, tantrum or outrage.
Those who left did not always mourn.
Pity was the best many could manage.
He had a stroke without warning,
maiming one side and locking him

to a wheel chair and one hand.
He died mute.
She died as silently one morning.
She had said once that she could not live without him,
proving that clichés are sometimes true
but they were embarrassing buddies
who had outlived their time.

ALIEN ACCEPTED

As I grow older and I hope wiser
 I feel as if I am visiting from another planet.
These extra-terrestrials who
fill the news and the streets
of this more and more exotic world
are not of my kind and it
is not clear which of us is
from outer space or some
satellite circling this dying
world which they call The Earth.
They often look like me
although thinner from running
or biking in gleaming packs
except also for a growing number
of those who appear to be
inflated beyond understanding
by some ingenious insidious
filler of gas or plastic stuffing
brain belly and butt whether fat or thin
as if they have been manufactured
in some far eastern factory by
robotic workers underpaid and
perpetually hungry and underfed.
Their ideas when I can discern
them are remote from reason
and seem from some exotic faith
bred into them before birth in
the womb of a strange being
neither male nor female

for the mystery remains as to
how I got here in this strange
planet called Wonderland

AT THE BIRD FEEDER

gold finches surround the seed[
darting and dashing as if the bright
yellow forsythia twigs had broken
loose from the background bushes
and animated with enthusiastic
feathered fowl life joined the birds
in their aerial dance of appetite
satisfaction mixed with happiness
as though bush and bird were
second cousins at the best if not
siblings from the same family

BELIEVING

There is this woman who talks to some God
every morning as robins greet the sun
she speaks to Him in capital letters.
She believes He is there and listens.
Sometimes lying next to her husband
who breaths quietly in and out,
she prays for the sick and for herself.
Sometimes she is alone in the warmth
of the bed, cradled in muslin sheets,
while her husband inhabits the kitchen,
having awakened with the Robins and Crows
and in answer to the cravings of his stomach.
Either way, she converses as if the Heavenly
switchboard had put her through directly
to Him who listens but does not speak.
There is no dial tone so she feels connected.
Eventually, she rises from the bed,
resurrected for another day as robins
muse about worms and the solar system
which they cannot name but accept
with no question without an identify.
She is a good woman but does not
have proof her conversation works
and in believing thinks that is all
there is needed as she goes on
performing her daily everyday tasks

AN OCCASIONAL DEER

comes out of the woods
edging our mowed lawn
but never when it is being
noisily trimmed by the tractor
mower expensively purchased
from the local Home Depot
but usually when one of the
family is soaking in the sun
and we wonder what this nearly
a fawn seeks that drives
him from the sanctity of our
Maine woods for we have
nothing to feed it but the wild
flowers in season and if we
call out it pauses to look
briefly at the caller and then
ducks its head and retreats
into the welcoming woods
where it is the ruler and
not a temporary resident who
owns the land for the moment

THE FOX

He cocked his head as if
to say and then ? while being
told a bit of gossip from
the neighborhood and waited
as he sat on the lawn two
houses down from ours but
we had no tale to tell that
might intrigue a red fox
but there are a few chickens in
only one yard on our street
mostly squirrels and chipmunks
stealing from the bird feeders
and Mother Nature appears
benign in this domestic setting
amongst the mix of small
cottages and the new mini-
castles blooming in the upscale
suburb on the edge of Casco Bay
as wealth moves in and edges
out the lobsterman who owns
that lawn and may succumb
to the urge to better his economic
status to one that impresses
even a wild red fox who is
seeking answers to some animal
question which we humans
don't know to ask but just
speculate about the urges
of the other residents of our street

CENTRAL PARK

He watches from the disciplined underbrush,
canine eyes and sharp muzzle
taking in city sounds, sights and stench.
Fifth avenue hums with buses and taxis
as background music.
The other boundary,
Eighth Avenue, masquerading as
Central Park West in the blocks
along the park
that really matter in our elite scheme of things,
echoes those city sounds
as this displaced coyote contemplates
small dogs and pigeons
for a necessary metropolitan meal.
Panic prevails in the city.
Pigeon lovers,
owners of small dogs,
cry for help over cell phones to 911 and 311.
Blue uniforms converge,
followed by the animal warden.
Swimming, or loping along a bridge,
the beast has invaded the city.
Civilization mobilizes its forces
in the face of incursion by the untamed.
The creature with pricked ears
moves from bush to tree to undergrowth
and is cornered by cop and tranquilizer gun.
Doped and caged, nature will be banished
to the forever wild

parklands
of upstate New York.
Pigeons, small dogs and in-line skaters
are safe once again.

A VIEW FROM THE ACADEMIC IVORY TOWER

There is no Rapunzel here but there are many others
who will gladly let down their hair
if there is a joke behind the act,
or a promotion or tenure or all three.
Clearly there are many jokes lurking
in the abstruse air of the academic
where genius is a term tossed about
as easily as juggling ten pins,
and prizes or publication can be found
it one is willing to turn over the rocks
and not mind the salamander or night-crawler
that might be revealed instead.
All in a day's work,
filling the heads of students,
like pouring milk into a glass
until it rises to the level of their eyes.

WATCHING THE WRITER DIE

in public or at least in print
the symptoms revealed
the treatment at hospice
outlined as well as the panic
that descends to the bottom
of his being when breathing
is not easy and when
falling and breaking occurs
without warning while the
crumbling bones only add
to the malevolent cells running
wild through the animal
body while the mind maintains
the clarity of knowing the
end is always death no matter
how long you manage to live

CONTRADICTIONS

It is too easy to notice faint chill
on the eyes in Autumn,
as though red and yellow of maples,
mahogany of oaks,
scarlet of euonymus,
move like breezes through the air,
and think
things are running down.
In fact,
sun warms deep into the bones,
while hint of ice on eyelids
startles the body
into alertness.
We watch children kick through leaves
as they rise, blown by whirlwinds.
Birds, agitated by abundance of seeds,
swoop and twitch from feathery flower heads
to opening pods heavy on Rose-of-Sharon.
Squirrels race from acorn to acorn,
pawing grass and ground,
overcome by appetite and affluence,
hiding and eating alternately.
Harvest overwhelms hibernation
to come,
at this moment
life bursts out of fruits' center
as if it were a kind of Spring again.

THE CRITIC'S TALE

had already begun when they met
and he was greatly impressed
by her step-mother who was a star in
producing and directing legit
dramas in an academic setting with
aspiring actors studying at elite
colleges where drama was a
popular and prestigious major
even as many starved in the Great
Depression for artists had to eat
as well as the common worker
so he married this relative child
to join the prestigious family
even though the bride was a short-
haired boyish young woman who
had yet to experience adult relations
on either an emotional or physical level
even though the marriage produced
to her joy twin boys but as they grew
the Critic became more famous
in his connections and found himself
wooed by handsome young men
impressed to be noticed by this
high-class famous reviewer of the arts
and his true male desire surfaced in the
relationships and a love affair with a
a woman seemed outlandish so
he turned away from the becoming
mother and adult female for his

true passion with a new beautiful
young man to replace the boyish
child who was growing into a real
woman before his amazed perspective
that he was a real father by accident
and he departed with his passionate
comrade to live in harmony away from
the ordinary family life with accidental
children and no domestic life with
mother and children but a gay life into
old age and fame as an eminent scholar
and grumpy drama critic

MY GRANDAUGHTER HAS DECIDED

she is not my granddaughter any longer
although in her discovery she is also
not my grandson either and wants to
be referred not as she or he or him or her
but them and their in clear violation of
standard grammatical usage but a linguistic
scholar has suggested in a letter to the New York Times
"one" could be used with clarity and in keeping
with standard English grammar although in
realizing neutral gender do not use sex
which seems to be a concept too prickly
than just gender which does not suggest the
damp and slippery moisture of cohabitation
and desire when she wishes to crop her <u>coiffure</u>
in ways despite her desire she appears closer
to being an adolescent boy than the female
person she clearly is attempting to escape

THE POET HAD FAITH IN FORM

for he knew that without form
it was not poetry
since his masters of the genre
preached with the sonnet or
the villanelle where control of
form was mastery of the poem
and therefore, of life itself
and even the <u>Limerick</u> design or the
simple couplet was a serious
poetic device when in the hands
of the significantly creative poet
although an unsophisticated aspiring
bard cannot substitute form for
a simple mind and construct an inspired
original perspective to create a poem
that is unique and complex for
intelligence is vital for authentic creativity
and an Emersonian impulse cannot
provide the truth that intellect seeks

OLD NUN IN THE SUPERMARKET

Counting the money carefully,
she watched the cash register
as each new item was recorded,
holding in a wrinkled shaking
hand a packet of dollar bills.
Stooped, she had to look up
from her bent aged back
to see the items rung up on
the super-market machine
that added her purchases one
by one as she lifted each
from the cart she clung to
with the empty hand as if
to a disabled person's walker.
Her gaze shifted from register
to cart as one by one she
lifted her items into the hands
of the very young girl who
tended the check-out,
rather than placing each item
on the ever-moving belt to
deliver her purchases into
the clerk's hands, who instead
were accepting each article,
until in a simple voice and with
an upheld hand, the nun said,
"enough," and let the burly male
packer empty the rest of the rejected
purchases as obvious beyond

her budget and the cash available.
God's budget had reached
the maximum for this day or
the modest amount tendered
to the checker in the ancient fist.
"Thank you, Ma'am," she said.
"And have a nice day."

MINORITY REPORT

There is something about Maine,
where the term "moderate" sounds so liberal,
where Ohio and Wisconsin displaced,
collide with New England and New York,
where country fiddle and jazz saxophone
ride over each other in raucous duet, with the harmonica,
where hybrid autos, SUVs, massive vans and pickup trucks
jostle for parking spaces at the Mall,
where mammoth mini-castles loom over
the modest home of the local lobsterman
and are in constant upgraded flux
for resale by Sotheby Real Estate as if each were a piece
of modern art, the shark in formaldehyde, and the ocean view
is for sale in the multi-millions,
where the local hayseed, deeply suspicious of those
from away, mixes with the sophisticates
who flee to Florida's sunny tax haven come the bad weather,
or have struck it rich in the local real estate market,
and hire the lawn services who clog Shore Road with
multiple mowers, services manned by men who plow
driveways in the off-season. and fish or lobster
when the prices are right,
where the organic farmers mingle with foodies who have
the money and time,
where scholars not tapped by the Ivy League hunker
down in Machias, in Presque Isle, or Farmington, and Fort Kent,
places known only to denizen Down-Easters,
where they can assume that envious role as resident scholars
at outposts of academia for mostly the locals who want

a job and do not read unless it is compulsory,
who are forced off the road by runners, and bikers
who are firmed, where the Bushes and their ilk,
play only minutes away from wheel-less trailers occupied
by forlorn folk, who, unlike those of neighboring
New Hampshire, live free *and* die.

WORLD CUP

The world goes crazy
in devotion to balls bouncing
from heads and feet
as if biting and clawing
contestants for that
elusive fame and fortune
one hears so much about
are eternal supermen,
with cerebral contributions
to make as the ball bashes
the brain from side to side
turning it to gray jelly
that cannot think straight
Given the devotion paid
to these amusements
as if games were the
reason for human existence,
one wonders if anyone
notices the poor, the homeless,
the hungry, the insignificant
crowded out of the picture
filled instead with double-
dealing players willing
to shave a score for gamblers'
payoff since winning the
game is not as important
as winning the big bet.

ONE-SIDED CONVERSATION WITH A SNAKE

The narrow fellow slides
over my garage floor,
surface unnatural for serpents,
even the minute garden variety.
Searching perhaps for an Adam
or an Eve, or more likely,
Emily Dickinson who would
not have been comfortable
in my dusty garage with
tools hanging from pegboard
and my Japanese car settling
in like some immigrant trying
to become as American as
this humble house in the suburbs.
Are you lost, my slippery friend,
or have you abandoned the garden
where organic vegetables thrive
but apple tree produces crabbed fruit
good only for jelly?
There is no answer beyond the
wiggle of a thin tale and a glide
through the corner of the door
and disappearance into the flowers
and ferns edging the driveway.
It is best not to stay where you
do not belong and to seek the familiar.

OBIT

According to a human interest
story in the local paper,
a retired real estate agent
died
when his golf cart
veered off the fairway
and
plunged over a cliff
to crash on a highway below.
Perhaps his last
thought
before crushing death
was
I should have spent more time
at the office.

FATAL

Pierre Curie and his wife, Marie,
worked on radioactivity
and for that work,
with a colleague,
were awarded the Nobel Prize in Physics.
Pierre was killed while crossing the street,
such a banal fate for such an exceptional man.
Marie died of a fatal version of anemia
due to radiation exposure.
Her cookbook is still so highly radioactive
that it is kept in a lead-lined box
and anyone wanting to read it
must wear protective clothing.
What would one prepare from that deadly domestic volume?
Gaining knowledge may be lethal,
not only to innocence,
but to life itself.
Be careful with what you half learn.

BURNING BUSH

the woods along the trail
are November lifeless
trees mostly leafless
or in the deep brown
dress of the oaks'
dead leaves as exception
brightening the under-
growth are the euonymus
shrubs a near scarlet
in the shadows of
this second growth
forest of oaks and maples
in the midst of death
or hibernation the
burning bush promises
a return of life in
the Spring that must
come after the sham
death of winter

GROUNDED

There has been a large outboard motor launch
in my neighbor's yard for the four years
I have lived next to it and its plastic cover.
It has never been any nearer to Casco Bay
than the length of the block where we two live.
I seldom do more than nod to its owner
when he rides his tractor mower as it
weaves over his yard and chews grass
that grows up to the immobile tires of the boat trailer
which are very flat and obviously not road ready.
He nods back and maybe smiles or maybe not
but just sweats in the summer heat when he
could be out in the ocean breezes in that
yard bound boat which never rocks or rolls
as a tide goes in and out or storms conjure
up mighty breakers that can be heart crashing
against the Maine rocks at the end of our street.
If that boat could have a soul would it
be yearning for the open water and the spray
in the face while the gulls soared and laughed
in circles overhead and the horizon stretched
seemingly forever away from the moan of
the fog horn warning of the Cape Elizabeth shoals?

THE STREET IS EMPTY

for it is the dinner hour
and one presumes families
are gathered around the table
as all good children are
for the evening meal which
they will eat everything if the
spinach is not to their liking
because plates should be
clean evening of gravy
in the disciplined families
who occupy this suburban
street where the gardens and
middle class hedges are
carefully groomed by blue-
jeaned men in pick-up trucks
with trailers carrying the machinery
of landscaping which the aspiring
of these first-time homeowners
demands that they use the symbols
of rising middle class as they
escape the demeaning labor
of the employment they are escaping
for wages by the hour which
is so very demeaning in the new
home-owner character they now
are with a mortgage they can barely afford

LATE AUNT MARTHA

died as a young woman
with a devoted boy friend
who made her artistic gifts
in his workshop cut off
by World War One and the great
flu epidemic of 1918 killed
fifty million people worldwide
while a mere sixteen million people
were killed by the terrible war
and my father escape both terrors
but my mother never forgot
the loss of musical Aunt Martha
and my mother's piano had
to solo in family music nights
while Aunt Martha's violin languished
in the clothes closet that contained
1918 garments that her sister
my mother could not bring
herself to give them to the needy poor
of her church although she knew
that would be the earthly act of
the good Episcopal she knew she was
from birth without question as
part of the devout family who hated sin

WIDOWS

traveled in groups as if numbers
provided safety and excitement
and often exotic scenery from
along with tour boat desk view
of strange lands viewed sometimes
to the classic music played by
semi-pro musicians on the loose
or reveled in the gourmand food
of footloose chefs with a stationary
kitchen in some important city
but they cannot find available
widowers to pair up with these footloose
single women roaming the vacation
spots from Alaska to the Caribbean
with stopovers in such ports as
Portland Maine or a man-less
Florida port to take on not
widowers but tropical fruit for dessert

THE DOG ACROSS THE STREET

barks when it sees us
but it is at the same time
wagging a friendly tail
so what is the target here
of bark or wagging tale
of another alternative sort
marking beast a split personality
perhaps an animal to be
smiled at with a friendly wave
but nothing more intimate
for although this animal
is a family pet I am not of
his family and will not be
petting an unknown beast
who may be of psychotic breed
ready to defend his home base
against the foreign monsters
inhabiting the house across the street

IT IS ASTER TIME

and purple blossoms fill
the spaces at the edge of
our backyard in a flood
of lavender mixed with
the yellow of Goldenrod
in order to deny the
impending knowledge
that winter ice is waiting
just beyond the edge
of Autumn although
the pessimist knows
the flowerless Ragweed
hides its malevolent
pollen in the glamour
of flowering Fall and
the aware of nature's
mixture of good and evil
waits to loosen the
malevolent that hides
its dual nature from
the hopeful and innocent
and it does not need
bites of the apple to
introduce evil into nature

AS PARENTS GROW OLD

the children become parental
and one wonders if that is in
response to love or the desire
to take charge at last in the new
adult existence denied them by parents
with important lives where children
were loved but secondary to mature
careers which society demands
comes first for significance
and capital to invest for family
security and prestige for career
confidence that the present culture
makes unhappily necessary

ROLLER SKATES OF NATURE

and chipmunks seem ecstatic
as do the larger gray squirrels
but I roller skate as I walk
amongst the fallen in my blacktop
driveway as if I must become
a fancy dancer or ice skater that
performs in the rink for an
audience that expects to be
entertained and I worry I
may trip on the product of
natures excesses and break a hip

THE TERRACE IS EMPTY

except for the single buck deer
crossing in the dusk of the first
day of Autumn as the cold sun
goes down over the suburban
mansions at the edge of the
southern woods and there is only
the sound of someone playing on
the drum set without any sense
of rhythm so one would guess
it is the practice of some adolescent
for a school music class or the
personal satisfaction of creating
sound to fill the growing darkness
and the deer pauses a moment as
the traps rattle away in the dusk
and deer may be wondering if
he is in danger but the sound is not
of gunfire so after the moment
of pause the animal leaps a hedge
and vanishes where the only music\
is the rustle of oak leaves

THERE COMES A TIME

in old age when a question
seems obvious although not
welcome so what is the point
in continuing the journey that
trek into the future when even
walking seems a chore and
laborious task and yet it is
only the ordinary demands
of existence and there are
still the devotion for some
important people you love
and love you so you go on

HE WAS THE FIRST ITALIAN AMERICAN

although he did it for the Spanish queen
by leaving behind all those Spanish
names as if the Italians did not count
even though now there is a movement
to rename the holiday Indigenous Natives
Day to honor mislabeled American Indians
which is an inaccurate term as well
 everyone vying for the nationalistic tag
that justifies all those statues of Admiral
Columbus who did not discover the
land now named after that other Italian
explorer who hoped to be more exact
than adventurous Columbus who looks
now like some blowhard who might
run for the presidency of what ever
we call this stew not Irish who came
 later for our pan-fried Greek omelet of a land

THE YOUNG BULL MOOSE

sauntered the shore streets of
Portland City as if he owned
the view of Casco Bay that his
adolescent hormones told him
seek out a receptive lady moose
of any friendly age while human
pedestrians gawked at the unusual
site of nature moving out of the
woods to the paved human
city streets filled with the residents
of this sophisticated Maine
metropolis who did not expect
a genuine moose to parade the
streets and the green park where
humans lounged and sniffed the
salty sea air mixed with the auto
exhaust of pleasure and commerce

Look to Nature for Truth

In prose verse

we are often told as if it could speak to us with the vital message
of life's meaning but it has nothing to tell us for the language is
not ours any longer and we cannot translate this foreign tongue
into our lives even if Thoreau thought he could read a message in
the woods that surrounded Walden Pond when the real lesson
was from the people who lived in the town of Concord hiding
alone in an upstairs bedroom or walking the streets while consid-
ering the trap that was conventional faith for nature and its
animal tenants could not inform without a human mind inventing
the order that was mortal and analyzing the facts as neutral
science reveals them to the perceptive human mind for Darwin
discovered more than Thoreau observed

THE SUICIDE NEXT DOOR

He has passed on,
she said,
dead being a word forbidden
to her lips
apparently.
Bleed to death right in
the bathtub.
She shuddered
as she vomited those words
Who would have guessed
supermarket journalism
drama for the suburbs?
Three police cars,
a fire truck
and one ambulance clogged
the private way
as people excluded from the house
paced and hugged.
Dead.
Passed on.
How about passed over?
What would the obituary say?
The woman in the house,
his live-lover
staying the night again,
seemed to have slept through it all.
Now she treads the driveway in tight circles
when not held by friends.
The medical examiner must come

for it to be made official,
and then the hearse,
the plastic body bag,
the evacuation of the black vehicles
with the uniformed stunned
young representatives of the law.
A cat is forgotten, left behind for the SPCA.
No reasons are acknowledged
in the death notice of the local newspaper.
Maybe a lovers' quarrel.
As with that illicit word
– DEAD—
reasons remain unspoken by those who know,
if they do.
Life gone bad is enough to know.
No one wanted the cat.
Unloved?

TRAVEL

The dawn drawn auto driver flings
the Sunday New York Times
down my driveway while I sleep
but when I wake and retrieve the
blue plastic bagged multiple
sections of interest, I know one
thing that is always the same.
The Book Review section will be
nestled between the pages of the
the Travel tales luring readers
to the fun, the exotic, the historic
places in and outside of the U. S. A.
and folded in will be the analysis of
the latest fiction, non-fiction, history
mystery, children's books, and
even an occasional collection of
verse for the poetically minded.
Travel there as well as in those pages
surrounding not exotic geography
but in the important locale of imagination.
The tourist of the land is becoming
abhorred as at the least a nuisance
and at worst the intimidator of
the local population where peace
is the standard while life is calm
and reasonably predictable for
the mob scene that is the center
for the newly wealthy traveler
who does not travel in the mind

through those books reviewed
in the newspaper of record
bit only in the third dimension
of distraction as that journeying crowd
flees from thoughts and ideas
while desiring only diversion.

IN PORTLAND MAINE

Many galleries in town would not show nudes.
The owners told the artist,
tourists bring children in
and that would just not do,
to have small children inspect bodies
in that state of undress.
They might not mind,
since children are inevitable curious,
about their bodies,
and how they are used in love,
but some of the parents
we get in town on vacation to see
the Maine coast, take the obligatory photo
with the Portland Head Light in the background,
are from the south,
you know,
the bible belt,
tour buses and tour boats
or vans with out-of-state licenses,
spew them out into the old port
to hunt for bargains
to show they have been somewhere,
and they want their children not exposed
(oh that word)
to naked bodies,
genitals even.
Horrors.
So we cannot hang your nudes
or exhibit your carvings

in a family oriented gallery such as ours.
I am sure you understand.
Do you have some nice paintings of flowers,
perhaps,
or shore scenes with crashing waves
maybe with a gull or two?
You know what I mean.

HUNTING SEASON

opens for the meat lovers
and the gun lovers
as well as the lovers
of thrashing dying deer
and innocent citizens
are warned about the
danger such aficionados are
for the harmless walkers
of the woods who would
not look good strapped
to the roof of the hunters
auto as the trophy of
the misguided hunt brings
home the mistaken prize
from the suburbs rather than
from the forest primeval

ONE WAITS FOR THE ILLUMINATION

that a poem might bring
if the poet is tuned in on
the right wavelength
and has a receiver that works
but unfortunately that is
not always the case
so the seeker looks and
listens for the right voice
and the lucky time and
sometimes a message breaks
through and listening is
rewarded for the painful
silence of the past